Island of Skorpa from Løsetstranda

Fjord Norway

An Adventure for Everyone

Kom forlag as
post@komforlag.no
www.komforlag.no
© Kom Forlag

Author: Olav Grinde
Main photographer: Per Eide
© Olav Grinde and Per Eide
Project Coordinator: Svein Gran
Graphic Design: Milla;Design

Other photographers:
Willy Haraldsen p: 12, 32
Tom Schandy/ Samfoto p: 69
Egil Korsnes p: 59
Troldhaugen Edvard Grieg Museum p: 62

Printed by: AIT Otta
Printed on 150 g Artic Volume

ISBN 978-82-92496-95-4

OLAV GRINDE   PER EIDE

FJORD NORWAY
AN ADVENTURE FOR EVERYONE

Kom forlag

IT IS THE DREAM

It is the dream we carry
that something wonderful will happen,
that it must happen —
that time will open,
that our hearts may open,
that doors shall open,
and the mountain shall open
that springs will gush forth —
and that our dream will open,
and that one morning we'll glide
into a cove we didn't know.

— OLAV H. HAUGE
(tr. Olav Grinde)

The translation of Olav H. Hauge's poem is printed by kind permission of Bodil Cappelen.

THE LYSEFJORD

THE DRAMATIC LYSEFJORD is a fjord unlike any other. Ten thousand years ago, at the end of the last ice age, the Lysefjord was an ice-filled valley. When the abrasive power of the ice cut the last threshold and the ice melted, the sea came flooding in. Without the supporting ice, the mountainsides soon began to crack, leaving sheer cliffs. The most impressive of these is Pulpit Rock, which rises 600 metres above the fjord.

When you peer up from the deck of a sightseeing boat, you might be surprised to hear that there is an easy trail to the top. On a clear day the view is unforgettable! Farther inland, on the southern shore, Kjerag is almost twice as high, a favourite amongst hikers as well as base jumpers.

Also on the southern shore is old Flørli Power Station. If you have the stamina, you can climb 4444 steps up the mountain, probably the longest stairs in the world.

Should you travel the Lysefjord by ferry, you have another climb ahead of you from Lysebotn, the village at the head of the fjord. The road ascends through 27 hairpin turns and continues over the mountains to Sirdal.

Hikers peering 600 metres down into the fjord. Below Pulpit Rock the Lysefjord is 422 metres deep.

Kjeragbolten – a boulder wedged into a crevasse a thousand metres above the fjord!

THE HARDANGERFJORD

THE SHELTERED SHORES of the Hardangerfjord are lush and fertile. They are at their most magical when the apple blossoms unfold in May. The fruit orchards along the fjord seem to consist entirely of white and pinkish flowers that compete in glory with the dazzling glacier and snow-topped mountains above. We can thank the Cistercian monks who planted the first apple seeds at Opedal in the Middle Ages.

As you follow the scenic road or sail into the fjord and fjord arms, you pass many villages. It's hard to pick out just one to visit; they all have their own charm – Utne, Ulvik and Eidfjord, Strandebarm and Norheimsund, to mention a few! Visiting the Barony in Rosendal and its Renaissance and rose gardens for the first time is like rediscovering a wonderful old memory.

If you are lucky enough to see a traditional wedding, be sure to catch the details of the colourful costumes. A Hardanger bride is a fairy-tale princess – when she weds, she even wears a golden crown!

Ferry at Utne. Fruit farm by the Sørfjord. Flowering apple orchard, Ulvik. Fjord idyll at Børsheimsholmen.

THE NÆRØYFJORD

ONE OF THE ABSOLUTE HIGHLIGHTS of a visit to Fjord Norway is a boat trip on the Nærøyfjord. This magnificent fjord is the narrowest in the world and a UNESCO World Heritage Site. Departing from the village of Gudvangen at the head of the fjord, the sightseeing boat passes meadows, woodlands and mountains that rise to 1200 metres. At Styve the fjord is only a few hundred meters across, and near the idyllic village of Nærøy it's not much wider.

On the mountainsides you may see sure-footed goats making their way to something green and edible, and from the nearby waters perhaps porpoises keeping a careful watch on the advancing boat. The landscape has seen little if any change since the Viking Age. The scenery is already dramatic at Beitelen, where the Nærøyfjord joins the Aurlandsfjord, another branch of the greater Sognefjord system. Perched on a mountain ledge near Beitelen is Stigen farm. Here the youngest children had to be secured with a leash, lest they fall into oblivion. Stigen means ladder – which could be pulled up when the tax collector came.

The Aurlandsfjord continues past the village of Undredal and its tiny white stave church, to Flåm. From this fjordside village you can embark on your next adventure – perhaps a kayak trip, a hike in the mountains or a ride on the Flåmsbana railway.

Anchored at Gudvangen. Beitelen, entrance to the Nærøfjord. Pastures near Gudvangen. The fjord narrows at Styve.

THE SOGNEFJORD

THE SOGNEFJORD EXTENDS from the open sea and halfway to the Swedish border, branching out into many scenic fjord arms. Along the shores of the Sognefjord are numerous charming villages, including Vik on the southern shore, Fjærland in a northern fjord arm, and Lærdalsøyri far inland, one of the best-preserved villages in Norway. Kaiser Wilhelm II was visiting a friend in picturesque Balestrand when World War I broke out. When the Norwegian government ordered him to leave, he took his time enjoying the view and his tea – before ordering full steam out the fjord just before the deadline.

You may well wish to follow his example, extend your holiday and savour nature's offerings. Those wishing to slow their pace may choose to hike the mountains along the fjord. As elsewhere in Norway, there are many mountain lodges. If the Sognefjord were drained of water, and you stood at its deepest point, you would be 1308 meters below sea level and peering up at mountains more than three kilometers high! You could spend months exploring this area.

Four of Norway's stave churches stand on the shores of the Sognefjord, while a fifth, Borgund, stands 27 km inland from Lærdalsøyri. The most famous of them all, and the oldest, is Urnes.

The Sognefjord is perhaps best experienced by boat. You may, however, consider portioning up the rewarding journey on Europe's longest fjord.

The Aurlandsfjord, one of many scenic fjord arms.

THE FLÅMSBANA RAILWAY

RAILWAY CONNOISSEURS consider Flåmsbana one of the most exciting railway rides in all of Europe, and rightly so. The initial stretch after you leave Myrdal station may seem ordinary, but the drama begins as soon as the train starts its descent of the Flåm valley. The railway line traverses deep canyons, hugs mountain shelves, speeds in and out of tunnels, passes snow-topped mountains and offers lush views of the green valley below.

Flåmsbana is a masterpiece of engineering and an impressive testimony to the endurance of the workers who spent 20 years constructing this branch line to the Bergen Railway. The Flåmsbana railway passes through 20 tunnels, most of which were cut with chisel and hand-drill through some of the hardest rock in Western Norway. There is even a tunnel in which the train turns 180 degrees inside the mountain!

The journey is a glorious, constantly changing 40-minute panorama. The difference in altitude between Myrdal and Flåm is 865 meters, giving this 20-kilometre journey a gradient of up to 1:18 and making it one of the steepest adhesion railways in the world.

It's a railway adventure worth repeating, so consider booking a return ticket.

Cruise ship at Flåm. Cycling the Navvies' Road (Rallarvegen).

THE GEIRANGERFJORD

THE DRAMATIC GEIRANGERFJORD does not start at the sea, rather it is merely an inner arm of a larger fjord system. It has enchanted travelers from around the world ever since the first tourist ship sailed into the fjord in 1869. Take a fjord cruise from Ålesund, or drive and take an extended ferry ride from one of the fjordside villages – you will soon appreciate why the Geirangerfjord is listed as a UNESCO World Heritage Site.

Snow-capped mountains, cascading waterfalls and lush vegetation clinging to the dark mountainsides are reflected in the tranquil waters of the fjord. Perched on mountain ledges are the farms of Skageflå, Knivsflå and Blomberg. Perhaps some of our folk songs were composed to court a beloved from a distance?

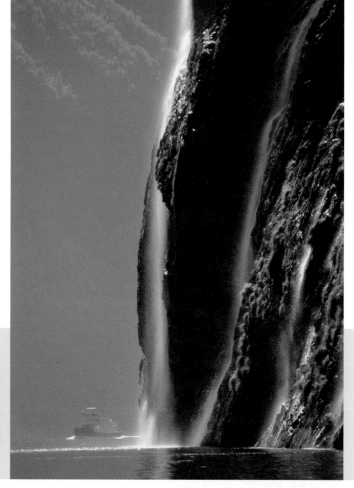

Skageflå farmstead. Viewpoint on Eagle Road. Brudesløret falls. Blomberg farm.

THE ICE THAT SCULPTED THE FJORDS

A SHEET OF ICE UP TO THREE KILOMETRES thick once covered most of northern Europe. It was this ice that carved out the magnificent fjords and deep U-shaped valleys of western Norway, scouring the land clean, patiently gnawing at mountainsides, relentlessly using the sand and rocks beneath the ice as an abrasive. That takes time and didn't happen during the most recent ice age. There have been a series of at least 40 ice ages over the last 2.5 million years, the most recent one ending about 10 000 years ago.

It has been calculated that ice carved away 5400 cubic kilometres to form the Sognefjord alone! Even so, the ice worked slowly, taking perhaps a thousand years to gnaw away a humble half metre of bedrock. In some places you can see the gouges and scratches made by the ice high on the mountainsides. In other places, the glaciers have deposited large quantities of gravel and rock transported by the ice.

There are over 30 glaciers in Norway, many of them in Fjord Norway. The Jostedal icecap, covering approximately 490 km², is the largest glacier on mainland Europe. Equally famous are three of its tongues: Briksdalsbreen, Nigardsbreen and Bøyabreen. Other major glaciers in the four western counties include Folgefonna and Hardangerjøkulen.

Exhibitions at the Norwegian Glacier Museum in Fjærland, at Breheimsenteret Glacier Centre in Jostedalen and Jostedalsbreen National Park Centre near Strynsvatn tell the story of the icecap and of the people who first dared to explore it. Glaciers are highly sensitive to climate change and the amount of snowfall, retreating or advancing with changes in temperature or precipitation.

The adventurous may spend a few hours wandering on one of the glaciers with an experienced guide. But never approach the ice without a guide – not unless you want a true once-in-a-lifetime experience!

Nigardsbreen. Guided glacier walk on Briksdalsbreen.

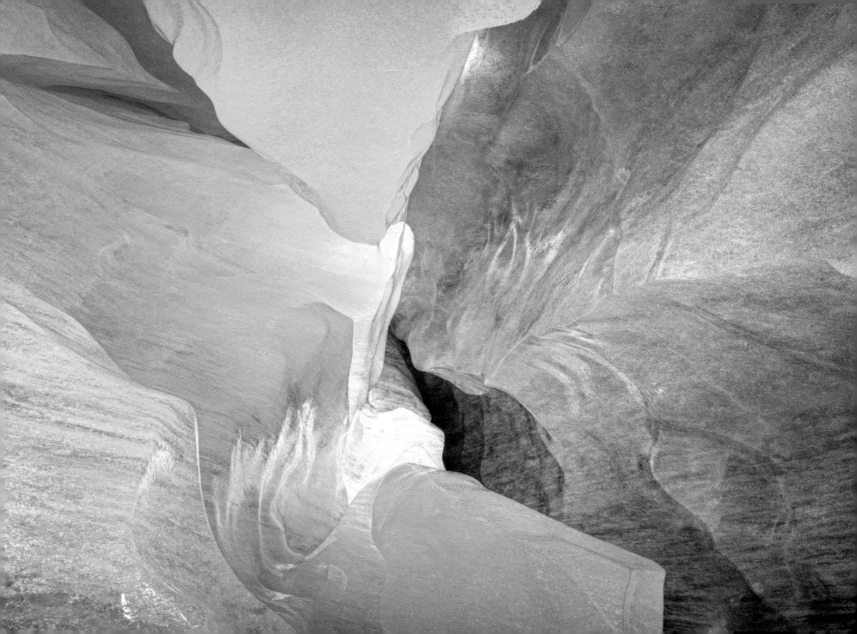

WATERFALLS

ON YOUR TRAVELS THROUGH FJORD NORWAY, you will see many raging rivers and impressive waterfalls. In fact ten of the world's 35 tallest waterfalls are situated in Norway's four western counties! This includes Vinnufossen, the highest in Europe.

Two of the most photographed waterfalls are De syv søstre (the Seven Sisters) in Geiranger, and Kjosfossen falls by Flåmsbana Railway. CNN Travel rates Langfoss by the Åkrafjord as one of the ten most beautiful waterfalls in the world. Other famous falls include Vøringsfossen, Mardalsfossen, Vettisfossen and Tvindefossen. You can actually walk *behind* Steinsdalsfossen near Norheimsund!

Thanks to its mountainous terrain and plentiful precipitation, Norway is well supplied with environmentally friendly hydropower. The Norwegian Museum of Hydropower and Industry in Tyssedal near Odda documents the fascinating pioneering days of this industrial history. To minimise environmental impact, most modern hydropower stations are actually built inside the mountain.

You may hear Norwegians complaining about the rain. One story has it that an exasperated tourist asked a young boy whether it ever stopped raining in Bergen. "I don't know, I'm only six years old," came the reply.

Hesjedalsfossen. Vidfoss in Sandvedalen. Vøringsfossen. The Seven Sisters.

URNES STAVE CHURCH

ON A SMALL HEADLAND overlooking an arm of the Sognefjord stands one of the world's foremost cultural monuments – Urnes stave church. Its excellent condition is fine testimony to the skilled craftsmen that built this church more than 800 years ago.

Time-honoured techniques of Viking boat-builders were used to prepare materials. Years before the felling of slow-growing pines, the tops would be cut off, filling the wood with resin and making it very resistant to rot. In addition stave churches were regularly treated with tar.

On our most complex stave churches – such as Urnes, Borgund and Hopperstad – we see gable upon gable rise to a crowning spire, giving them their very characteristic shape. The stave churches' elevated naves, arcades and columns ending in cubed capitals are reminiscent of Romanesque stone churches. Some experts, however, are convinced that their architecture is based on the pre-Christian style and construction methods of the Vikings.

The stylised and intertwined animal carvings of the Urnes portals bear a remarkable resemblance to the ornamentation of the Irish Book of Kells. Irish monks travelled to Norway centuries before 1030, the date officially used for the introduction of Christianity, and Vikings brought back Irish slaves and craftsmen on their journeys.

It is estimated that 2000 stave churches were built in the period 1150–1350, an average of ten per year. Evidence suggests that stave churches were prefabricated and the standardised parts quickly assembled by specialised craftsmen. The use of staves to build self-supporting walls was once a common construction method throughout much of northern Europe.

Today, there are 28 stave churches left, most of them in Norway's four western counties. In addition, the stave church at Fantoft outside Bergen, which burned down in 1992, has been painstakingly rebuilt using traditional techniques.

Carved door and portal at Urnes, a UNESCO World Heritage Site. 140 portals have been wholly or partly preserved.

BRYGGEN *and the Hanseatic merchants*

ALONG THE HARBOUR, the distinctive row of gable-end buildings glows in the sun. The 58 remaining buildings represent an architectural tradition that dates back almost 900 years. Such wooden frontages were once a common sight in many European harbour towns.

Bryggen is a national treasure included on UNESCO's World Heritage List. Artists and craftsmen, translators and fashion designers, architects and stone sellers now occupy the workshops and stores where Hanseatic merchants once kept dried fish and other goods. There are also cosy pubs and first-class restaurants with dangerously sloping original floors.

The narrow wood-paved passages between the deep buildings invite you away from the harbour, as though to pull you deep into Bryggen's past. Bryggen was the economic centre of Bergen from the time the city was founded in around 1070. From 1360, Hanseatic merchants dominated Bryggen's commercial and social life; at times there were as many as 2000 Germans residing in Bergen, mostly involved in the export of dried fish. For centuries, services in German were held in the nearby St. Mary's Church, the oldest in Bergen, built in the mid 12th century.

Seven major fires have caused much destruction. After each fire, Bryggen was rebuilt in accordance with the original pattern. The present buildings date back to 1702. In 1955, a devastating fire destroyed nearly half of the buildings. Archaeologists used the opportunity to dig down into the layers underneath the ashes. At Bryggen Museum at the north end of Bryggen, these finds are preserved – ceramics and glass from many countries of the Continent attest to trade links as early as the 12th century.

"Statsraad Lehmkuhl" and a restored pivot crane. The Fortress. An old ledger at Hanseatic Museum. Glimpses from Bryggen.

BERGEN – *the City of Seven Mountains*

ROME MAY BE built on seven hills, but only Bergen has the distinction of being surrounded by seven mountains. When the sun breaks through the cloud cover, Bergeners forget that it may have rained for days on end. For summer visitors, the weather gods seem to clear the sky of clouds. Regardless of the season, the approach by sea is unforgettable.

Bergen is sometimes referred to as "Norway's secret capital". For centuries it has been the most cultural and international city in the country. Art lovers will be pleased that there is an enviable concentration of museums around the central lake. Bergen is notable for its wooden architecture. Over the last couple of decades, hundreds of old wooden houses in the Sandviken and Nordnes areas have been lovingly restored.

You may notice tens of thousands of rhododendron blossoming along the thoroughfares of Bergen. Most were donated by a wealthy businessman who wished to share the fruits of his labour.

In the 19th century, other town patriots established Fjellveien (the mountain road), a fine promenade that you can stroll along at your own pace and absorb the impressions of the historic town below.

No visit to Bergen is complete without a bird's eye view. The Fløibanen funicular brings you up to a wonderful view of Bergen. Many people appreciate long walks in these mountains. Mount Ulriken, the highest of Bergen's seven mountains, offers a most magnificent panorama of the region.

If you see a traffic jam in Bergen, it may not necessarily be due to rush hour. Should you hear drumming, then it's almost certainly one of the "buekorps" marching, uniformed youth brigade complete with make-believe bayonets and cross-bows. Where else in the world can bands of juvenile boys march in the middle of the street, obviously taking their time, despite impatient drivers, without endangering their life and health?

Fløibanen funicular and view. Winter panorama. Rosesmauet. The harbour, peering up at Fløien and Mount Ulriken.

STAVANGER – *prosperity from the sea*

STAVANGER DATES ITS CITY STATUS 1125, around the time Bishop Reinald is said to have arrived from Winchester. He brought a large number of carpenters and masons with him from England and announced that he was going to build a cathedral by Breiavatn. Even so, for centuries Stavanger consisted of a small group of buildings around the harbour. As recently as 1800, the town had a population of only two thousand.

The population grew in the 18th and 19th centuries, thanks to the rich herring fisheries. This gave rise to a huge canning industry and considerable exports to the Continent. In Old Stavanger there are 173 workers' homes from this period, huddled along narrow cobblestone streets. This concentration of wooden buildings is one of the largest in Northern Europe, but it is not a museum; the little white houses are well kept by grateful residents who know how to appreciate the charm of this little town-within-a-town.

Many of the old canning factories are still standing, refurbished into upscale apartments and offices.

Outside Stavanger are petroglyphs and grave mounds that bear witness to a far older history. As long as 3–4000 years ago the chieftains of this area had strong links to continental Europe. At Hafrsfjord, southwest of the city centre, three enormous swords are stuck deep into the bedrock. They are a monument to Harald Fairhair and the battle he won here in 872 to unite Norway under his own rule.

On Christmas Eve 1966, oil was struck in the Ekofisk sector, and the North Sea once again became the source of prosperity – for Stavanger and all of Norway.

Stavanger Cathedral, the harbour, Norwegian Petroleum Museum, Old Stavanger.

ÅLESUND – *the Art Nouveau town*

THE TOWN OF ÅLESUND IS BEAUTIFULLY situated, facing the open sea. Perhaps nowhere else in the world do we find a more harmonious concentration of Art Nouveau architecture. For this we can thank the catastrophic fire of 1904, which left 800 buildings in ashes. Only one person perished. As the prison warden watched the flames approach, he was forced to release his 14 prisoners. As they ran for their lives he shouted, "Come back to-morrow!"

In just three years, architects and craftsmen from all over Norway rebuilt the town in an Art Nouveau style that borrows inspiration from Old Norse decorations. A visit to the Art Nouveau Centre will give added insight into this architectural history. For a bird's eye view, climb the 418 steps to the top of Aksla.

There is a standing joke about the thrifty, industrious and pious people of Ålesund and the Sunnmøre region: Should one of them be shipwrecked on a desert island, when you rescue him a month later he will have built a furniture factory and a chapel!

The fact of the matter is that this region accounts for more than three quarters of Norway's furniture industry. Ekornes still produces the famous Stressless chairs introduced in 1971, providing comfort for the weary backs of more than five million purchasers worldwide.

Raise your eyes to see the Art Nouveau town's amazing details! Brosundet – above and below the surface. Panorama from Aksla.

KRISTIANSUND – *klipfish and opera*

KRISTIANSUND, BUILT ON THREE ISLANDS located at a junction of fjords, is the northernmost town in Fjord Norway. When King Christian VI granted the settlement township status in 1741, against loud opposition from Bergen and Trondheim, the locals honoured him by renaming it Christiansund.

You don't see the fine natural harbour before you actually sail into it. This harbour is the true town centre of Kristiansund. The wharf here is from the 17th century and is 60 years older than the famous Bryggen in Bergen.

Herring was the most important catch in the 18th century. Fortunately, as herring catches dropped, the klipfish trade blossomed. The fish was skinned, split and salted before being dried on cliffs (*klipper*, hence the name). By 1790, the merchants of Kristiansund were exporting all they could produce and were sending schooners northward to Lofoten to buy more fish. By the 19th century, Kristiansund had become one of the most important export ports in Norway, and there was a growing class of wealthy merchants. Some of them were well-travelled and spoke four or five languages. The local dialect still contains Spanish words and audible influences from other countries. Considering her strong, continental bonds, it's not so strange that Kristiansund was the first Norwegian town to establish an opera – 32 years before our capital did.

In this day and age, few people reflect on the fact that the city lies 10 km from the mainland. In 1992, Kristiansund was linked to the mainland through Krifast, a road project that included the hundred-metre-high Gjemnessundet Bridge and a 5.1 km long subsea tunnel.

Almost two thirds of the city's buildings were destroyed in massive bombing between the 28th of April and 2nd of May, 1940. The people of Kristiansund have never sat around waiting for others to do things for them; as soon as they could start rebuilding, they contacted Sverre Pedersen, Norway's foremost city planner at the time. He and leading architects helped to create a new city, providing it with a clean, functionalist architecture.

The Opera. The harbour is the heart of Kristiansund. Bridge joining Kirkelandet and Innlandet. Nordlandet is the town's third island.

Valldøla – Norddal

RUNDE – *a paradise for birds*

IT'S QUITE A SPECTACLE to see tens of thousands of birds flying to and from their chosen spots on the 300-metre-high cliffs at Runde. With marvelous precision, the airborne parents momentarily return to feed impatient offspring who seem unaffected by the dizzying heights.

No other bird cliff is visited by more species; 240 bird species have been observed at Runde. The puffin is the most numerous of them all, with 100 000 couples nesting here. Every spring they are joined by huge colonies of kittiwake, auk, cormorants, guillemot, fulmar, petrel and gannet.

On the island of Runde there are wetlands where eider duck, shelduck and oyster catchers come to nest. Many smaller birds also thrive on the island.

For bird lovers and ornithologists, Runde is paradise – the most visited bird cliff in all of Norway. Wildlife managers have established numerous good observation posts. In spring and summer it is forbidden to enter the nesting areas.

Colourful puffin. Watchful eagles soar above curious kayakers.

THE ATLANTIC ROAD

IF ADVENTURE IS WHAT YOU'RE LOOKING FOR, here is some sound advice: choose only the roads that wind like rivers across the landscape, not those that seem drawn with a ruler. You may be astonished that your drive also becomes a journey back in time. The less direct route will wind its way past scattered houses, across stone bridges and past wooden boats, across mountain passes long since replaced by tunnels, and take you across narrow bridges to islands where a few dozen recalcitrant locals still insist on living year round.

One adventure not to be missed is the coastal drive from Molde to Kristiansund. The Atlantic Road skips elegantly from island to islet. Eight bridges take you across islands and skerries. With the fjord to your right and the open ocean to your left, you sometimes feel as though you're driving right on the water, especially on a windy day when breakers drench your car. Road workers endured 12 hurricanes to build this highway. In 2005 Norwegians voted the Atlantic Road the *Engineering Project of the Century*.

The road maps of other countries often label scenic routes. In Fjord Norway, there is the Hardanger Road, the Ryfylke Road, the North Sea Road, the road to Bremangerlandet, the old road across Strynefjell … Come to think of it, it's probably easier to make a list of the road sections that *don't* take you through magnificent scenery!

Bird's eye view, northern lights and storm at the Atlantic Road.

FACING THE SEA

THE COASTAL SEA ROUTE has been the main traffic artery in all but modern times. Whereas on land there are traces of old roads and trails dating back to Viking times, the wake of a boat leaves no trace. Instead, there are ancient harbours and old fishing villages, trading posts and old inns, the occasional written account and the evidence of place names.

Fishing villages were established so that fishermen could be as close as possible to the fishing grounds. When engines increased the reach of vessels, the most remote and exposed villages were gradually abandoned, with people moving onto the mainland or to more sheltered areas. Some of the settlements that once teemed with the activity of thousands of fishermen have found a new livelihood, while others today seem permanently asleep.

A number of these beautifully situated villages, however, have received positive attention and care in the past decade or two. Gradually houses have been refurbished, and it's not uncommon for Norwegian families or appreciative foreign tourists to rent them for a week or three.

There are many treasures – of which Sogndalsstrand, Espevær, Krosshamn, Glesvær, Kræmmerholmen and Fedje, Håholmen, Utvær, Bulandet, Bud, Ona, Grip and Veidholmen are only a selection.

All but a minuscule portion of Norway's gross national product is produced within a few kilometres of the coast or on the oil platforms offshore. That is why most of the villages and towns of the four counties of Fjord Norway still overlook the sea or fjord.

Coastal Museum at Herøy. Veidholmen on Smøla. Sogndalstrand in Rogaland. Ona village and lighthouse.

TROLLSTIGEN

ONE OF NORWAY'S MOST POPULAR attractions is Trollstigen, a stunning scenic road and an impressive feat of engineering. A series of 11 hairpin turns take you from the mountain to the valley floor, or vice versa.

In some places the road is cut into the mountain; in others it is built on top of stone support walls. King Haakon VII opened Trollstigen in 1936, after road-builders had toiled for eight years. One of their challenges was building the stone bridge that carries you across the 180-metre high Stigfossen falls.

From the two viewpoints at the top of Trollstigen, you can savour the sight of the surrounding mountains that rise to more than 1000 metres.

You may well experience the drive down the 11 hairpin turns as "mountaineering by car". It's a long way down to the valley floor, so please check that the brakes are in order and insist that your driver watch the road and not the magnificent view!

When you reach the valley below, do consider a short detour to the foot of Trollveggen, the tallest vertical rockface in Europe. When you finally arrive at the fjordside town of Åndalsnes, your satisfied family is likely to be grinning from ear to ear – and breathing a sigh of relief.

New buildings with restaurant and exhibition on Trollstigen and Norway's National Tourist Routes. Viewpoint above Stigfossen falls.

SELJA AND STAD – *storms and prayers*

SELJA SEEMS A DESOLATE AND UNSPOILED ISLAND. Only a handful of people live here year-round, wild goats feel at home on the rocky slopes and eagles guard her skies. But near the ruins of the monastery that played a vital role in the Christianisation of Norway, lay what was once the most important harbour between Bergen and Trondheim.

The Stad peninsula, immediately to the north, is like an arm and fist clenched in defiance of the Atlantic Ocean. Even before the Viking Age, ships sought safety on Selja when storms raged the dreaded waters around the peninsula – "the largest graveyard in Norway". Sailors would pray for safe passage, or wait until the storms abated. That could take weeks; a recent brochure for the area candidly advertised "Norway's fiercest and most frequent storms".

A few sailors who were less patient would actually drag their boats across the peninsula at a place called Dragseide. Today there is talk of building a ship tunnel to provide safe passage.

Cliffs at Stad. Panorama of Ervik. Selje monastery ruins. Old cemetery at Ervik.

Kannesteinen – Måløy

THE VIKINGS

BY AND LARGE, THE VIKINGS were peaceful, and most of the goods and treasures they brought home were acquired through honest barter. The Vikings' reputation as plundering barbarians is overstated. But all agree that they were amongst the finest boat-builders the world has seen – and they sailed far in their humble ships.

Leif Eiriksson reached America 500 years before Christopher Columbus. The Vikings settled Iceland and Greenland, Orkney and Shetland, the Faeroes and Hebrides, Normandy and much of the British Isles and Ireland. Dublin was founded by a Viking chieftain in 850.

The Norsemen navigated the Rhine, sailed up the Volga through Russia, all the way to the distant shore of the Caspian Sea, before crossing to Baghdad on foot. They passed through the Straits of Gibraltar, took service in the Imperial Guard at Constantinople, and reached the Holy Land. They acquired Arab glass, rich treasures of coins and silver, Persian ceramics and Irish bronze. They sold furs and honey, and utensils of soapstone.

The Viking Ship Museum in Oslo contains fine ships, a richly ornamented ceremonial carriage, horse sleds and many other treasures.

On the island of Karmøy in Western Norway, the carefully re-built Viking farm at Avaldsnes on Karmøy brings the culture of the Norsemen back to life.

Midsummer's Eve celebration by the Hafrsfjord Monument. Viking weapons and objects. Historical pageant at Herøy.

BOAT-BUILDING TRADITIONS

EVER SINCE THE VIKINGS SET SAIL in their longships, Norway has been justly famous for the excellent craftsmanship of its boat-builders. Petroglyphs and archaeological finds indicate that this tradition is far older than the Vikings, although they refined boat-building to a fine art. Anyone who visits the Viking Ship Museum outside Oslo will be struck by the elegance of their vessels. The smaller rowboats that were found with the Gokstad Ship bear a remarkable resemblance to the Oselvar, still being built in the district south of Bergen.

Hull designs and rudder fittings suggest that sails were not in use until the 8th century. That's almost four thousand years after the Egyptians and Mesopotamians made use of the wind – but the Norwegians caught on quickly and were soon sailing remarkably sturdy vessels far and wide.

We know from the sagas that ships as long as 40 metres were built for Olav Tryggvason. Many boats were built surprisingly far inland, near mature forests of slow-growth pines. The famous Oseberg Ship was built entirely of oak. Specially shaped materials were used as ribs and rowlocks. The boat-builders knew their forests well and could afford to wait for a tree with a desirably curved root or branch to reach its ideal size.

Preparation of materials would start even before a tree was felled. Perhaps the top of the tree was cut off, so that the trunk would fill with resin. Materials might be submerged in the sea or a marsh for a year or two, with those showing signs of rot being discarded. The most vulnerable places on a ship, such as the end grain of ribbing, were drilled and filled with sea salt to prevent rotting.

Many old ships and boats have been restored to seaworthiness at Mellomværftet, the boatyard at Nordmøre Museum in the town of Kristiansund, and at the Hardanger Vessel Preservation Centre in Norheimsund.

It's quite a sight when harbours are filled with old wooden boats. The Market Days (Torgdagene) in Bergen and the Harbour Days in Haugesund are just two such cultural events that are not to be missed!

Petroglyphs. The Market Day in Bergen attracts many wooden boats.

Juvatnet – Vanylven

Svinøy lighthouse

THE CULTURAL LANDSCAPE

FROM THE AIR, it may seem that Norwegians have left their mark on a mere fraction of the land. On closer inspection there are many traces.

The trained eye sees old hunting pits, vegetation changed by centuries of grazing near mountain farms, old burial mounds and outlines of the foundations of ancient dwellings. It makes out stone walls overgrown with moss supporting terraces of tilled land, slabs of slate leading across brooks to old elm trees with short trunks and many low branches that were once harvested for fodder, and crofts long since reclaimed by the forest.

Archaeologists have speculated as to why they haven't found more farms and settlements from the Viking period. The simple explanation may be that many contemporary farm buildings are built right on top of the old ruins.

A few old hamlets do remain, such as Agatunet and Havråtunet. In 1837, a new law radically changed inheritance rules, holdings were kept more intact and farmers moved their houses out of village clusters onto their own land.

The soil of the Norwegian coast is sparse and thin. Even cultivated fields are broken by boulders and crags, and between the fields are groves of trees that seem like remnants of an older landscape.

The vast heather-clad heathlands are not wilderness, but rather a man-made landscape that once stretched all the way from northern Spain to the Lofoten Islands. The Heathland Centre at Lygra, north of Bergen, provides insight into this heritage.

No one knows how many miles of rock walls divide up the coastal lands. There are endless volumes of local history detailing what is known about each farm. Of course the knowledge of our collective memory only stretches so far back into the mists of time. Much is waiting to be discovered even by the trained eye.

Old foundations in Lyngstøylsvatnet. Houses sheltered by Hellaren. Goats in Urkedalen. Fjordside village of Finnes. Norwegian Fjord horses.

EDVARD GRIEG *and the Hardanger fiddle*

MUSIC LOVERS the world over listen to the music of Edvard Grieg and picture in their mind's eye fjords and mountains, dark forests and crystal clear rivers, trolls, be-guiling milkmaids and lively dancing to the fiddle. His music is imbued with an unu-sually rich melodic expression and vitality.

Grieg's Opus 17, "25 folk songs and dances", was dedi-cated to Ole Bull, the famous violinist on whose recommen-dations he entered the Leipzig Conservatory. When Grieg visited the Hardanger area, he loved to listen to the many folk songs.

The double-stringed Hardanger fiddle has a sound that sets it apart from the violin. As the fiddler draws his bow across perhaps two or three strings, the sympathetic strings just under them resonate, lending the music an ethereal quality. Melody and drone are inter-woven in a magical tapestry of sound.

Perhaps that is what inspired the composer to transcribe many folk melodies and arranged piano music based on them. Most notable is Opus 72, which really should be heard juxtaposed with the fiddle music that inspired it. Grieg remained faithful to the dissonance of the Hardanger fiddle, and he managed to keep the rhythmic force of the fiddle intact.

At the age of 24, Edvard married his cousin, Nina Hagerup. Nina's mother, who was opposed to the marriage, protested that: "He is nothing and has nothing, and he writes music which no one wants to hear." Like many other mothers-in-law, she is now forgotten.

The very next year Edvard Grieg composed his masterpiece – the Piano Concerto in A Minor – one of the most frequently played piano concertos. Some years later, the playwright Henrik Ibsen asked him to write music to his dramatic poem, *Peer Gynt*. The resulting 26 compositions made the premiere of this work in 1876 a resounding success.

Grieg tuned his music to the spirit of the folk music tradi-tions. Today, much of the renewal of Norwegian traditional music happens at the cutting edge, when it meets other music forms, such as jazz and the folk music of other countries.

The double-stringed Hardanger fiddle is often richly ornamented.

WALKING THE MOUNTAINS

NORWEGIANS ARE WELL AWARE of their privileged surroundings and make good use of the wilderness. To accommodate them, the Norwegian Mountain Touring Association (DNT) has marked a fine network of thousands of miles of trails between their mountain lodges. These allow also tourists to explore the mountains of Fjord Norway.

But where to go? It's far easier to list the places in Fjord Norway devoid of mountains! From Kjerag or Pulpit Rock you can enjoy stunning views of the Lysefjord. The Geirangerfjord and many other fjords merit extended exploration. The town of Molde boasts a panorama of 222 peaks – take your pick! In Bergen, just take the funicular up to Fløyen or the cable car to Mount Ulriken and start walking, turning around now and again to enjoy the view of the "City of Seven Mountains".

Throughout Fjord Norway there are waterfalls to discover and mountain lakes teeming with trout. The wilderness is delightfully uncrowded – and in the summer you can enjoy it almost around the clock. How about being able to boast that you went skiing on a glacier? There are several summer ski centres where you can do just that.

More than a few Norwegians view the mountains as fixed points in their existence, and so return to them regularly for renewal. It's been said that when the church tries to count its congregation, it should include most of those who seek the silence of the mountains – after all, prayer is an act of the listening heart.

Mist over Sunnmørsalpene. Viewpoint at Skrednakken. Cabin in Breiedalen, Geiranger.

FISHING THE RIVERS AND SEA

IF YOU THROW A HOOK into the sea or fjord, you have to be quite unlucky not to haul up a catch. There is plenty of cod, saithe, haddock, mackerel and dozens of other species to satisfy everybody. The Gulf Stream sweeps warm waters toward the nutrient-rich coastal waters.

The importance of fish in Norwegian history can hardly be exaggerated. The towns of Haugesund and Stavanger are said to be built on herring bones. Bergen would not have become what it is today without the Hanseatic traders, who for centuries made fortunes exporting dried cod from Lofoten to the Continent. Many petroglyphs depict fish, and even the historians of ancient Greece found reason to comment on the unusually rich fishing in these waters.

In the middle of the 19th century, wealthy English adventurers discovered the huge salmon that migrated up the rivers of western Norway to spawn. They were astonished to hook specimens weighing more than 30 kilos. A few Scottish and English families still lease the exclusive right to fish certain stretches of the best salmon rivers during the summer.

Some of the best salmon rivers in the western counties are Bondalselva, Drivavassdraget, Gloppen, Gaula, Nausta and Flekkeelva, Daleelva, Oselva, Etneelva, Tengselva, Bjerkreimselva, Figgjo, Håelva and Ogna. Conditions change from year to year, and you would be well advised to book ahead.

Trout fishing is a far less costly sport than salmon fishing. In Norway, there are many rivers and tributaries, and thousands of lakes where you can enjoy solitude and magnificent scenery while trying your luck. More than a few chefs admit that the best way to enjoy trout is to cook it over an open fire, perhaps adding a few wild herbs. Even if none should strike at your line, you're more than likely to return with a satisfied smile at day's end.

Professional and amateur fishermen must be prepared for changeable weather – and a great catch!

TAKE THE CHALLENGE!

THERE IS GREAT SATISFACTION in taking the most challenging route, and reaching the summit. You will find excellent climbing in most parts of Fjord Norway. One of the best known is Trollveggen, a magnificent 1100-metre high cliff in Romsdalen. In 1967, French climbers used 20 days to ascend the direct route to the top! Not far from Trollveggen are the beautiful Sunnmøre Alps and the challenging Romsdal mountain range.

If you perch on a craggy peak and gaze down at the luminous sea of clouds flowing around the mountaintops nearby, you may feel as if you have grown wings! For some, the feeling is not enough – they stretch their wings to go paragliding or hang-gliding from mountain peaks.

A few years ago, Norwegian base jumpers had to keep their passion a secret or risk losing their parachuter's license. From the Kjerag in the Lysefjord, base jumpers can enjoy an impressive 20-second free fall. Karlsgråtind in Romsdal, much further north, is considered the safest site in Northern Europe, thanks to the large overhang and excellent landing conditions.

Rafting is one of the wildest ways to enjoy the foaming Norwegian rivers. You have to learn to "read the river" – it's no use fighting the force of the water. Team spirit is of the essence as you race down the waters in a raft, coordinating every movement. Among the best rivers are Raundalselva and Strandaelva, Jølstra and Breimselva. Brandsetelva has an impressive series of obstacles that make it ideal for extreme sport.

Experienced connoisseurs of water sports prefer the kayak. It responds far quicker, allows better control and brings you into closer rapport with the rushing river. Sea kayaking is less extreme, and there are plenty of fjords and coastal waters to explore, but do heed the weather forecast.

The week of Midsummer's Eve, Voss is the place to be. That is when the annual week-long Ekstremsportveko attracts practitioners of extreme sports from all over the world. Even spectators enjoy the adrenaline rush.

Rafting on Valldøla. Panorama at Kolåstind. Base jumper throws himself off Kjerag.

A DIVER'S DELIGHT

YOU MAY BE SURPRISED to hear that Norway has a reputation as one of the world's most exciting diving paradises. Underwater fjord views can be just as impressive as the landscape above the waterline familiar to tourists. Sheer cliffs plunge into black depths – Sognefjord is more than 1300 metres deep. Crevasses, screes and overhangs add to the underwater drama.

In their own way, our coastal waters can be as exotic as more tropical seas. Admire colourful sea anemones and watch plants sway in tidal currents. Explore the underwater caves at Stad. Bring up scallops and wolffish for a feast with friends.

There are still silver and gold coins to be found near the wreck of the "Akerendam", which sank near Runde in 1725. Here, in 1974, at a depth of less than ten metres, divers brought up more than 700 kilos of precious metals. Even if you don't discover gold, you may be lucky enough to see a puffin or cormorant dive for its dinner.

Hustadvika, between Molde and Kristiansund, is special for other reasons. Impressive underwater rock formations, a kelp forest, and the unusually varied fauna that includes a seal colony, have made this a favoured diving area. Numerous dive centres along the coast will be happy to provide equipment and point your way to great spots.

If you prefer to stay dry, you can get a good impression of the underwater Norwegian world by visiting the fine aquarium outside Ålesund or the one in Bergen.

Diver beneath the glacier, and at Hustadvika.
Next pages: Cod in kelp forest. Underwater cave at Stad. Male cuckoo wrasse. Exploring a shipwreck in Skatestraumen.

FESTIVALS *of Fjord Norway*

THE VIKINGS WERE GOOD at finding an excuse to hold a good feast or festival. When music was played and stories were told for days and nights on end, people would come from afar to join the fun. In that respect times haven't changed much.

Summer is the hottest festival season. For those who appreciate folk music, a highlight is the Førde Folk Music Festival. Stavanger is well-known for its International Chamber Music Festival, where some concerts are held in a 13th century monastery. The Bergen Festival dates back to a music festival that Edvard Grieg helped to organise in 1898. Parallel events include concerts of contemporary music and a jazz festival. When it comes to jazz, however, the town where it really swings is Molde, in mid-July.

There are also a number of historical pageants, most of them performed at outdoor sites where the events portrayed actually took place centuries ago – such as at Moster and Kinn.

Sting on outdoor stage at Romsdal Museum. Music and celebration in the streets during Molde International Jazz Festival.

NORWEGIAN CUISINE

NORWEGIAN CUISINE has progressed in leaps and bounds during the last 20 years. Whether a chef has a traditional approach, embraces impulses from abroad or brings his own twist, his dishes will be based on world-class ingredients. The agriculture here is one of the purest and cleanest in the world.

Traditional dishes generally don't complicate matters with fancy sauces or exotic herbs. Often the only seasoning added to fish is salt. Since the potato was introduced in the 18th century, it has been a staple of the Norwegian diet. Many preachers saw it as virtually their duty to spread the good news of this nourishing root.

Some travel guides suggest that tourists on a budget make do with one meal a day; a Norwegian breakfast buffet can make the continental croissant with jam seem like prison food. And the number of well-filled napkins that have found their way into the rucksacks of grateful backpackers is proof that breakfast really is the most important meal of the day.

Norway certainly has held its own ever since the biannual Bocuse d'Or, the culinary equivalent of the World Cup, was established in 1987. Only French chefs have garnered more gold medals. This has inspired many to renewed efforts in their kitchens, not least the chefs of some restaurants in Fjord Norway.

Of course, fancy cooking need not always be the answer. One of the easiest ways for a Norwegian to prepare a feast is to purchase several kilos of freshly caught shrimp, crusty white bread, mayonnaise and lemon – and tell the guests to bring wine and beer. A guaranteed success!

For dessert there are ingredients that require no preparation at all, only a refined hand-to-mouth movement. It is hard to imagine anything tastier than our sun-ripened strawberries in summer, or wild blueberries fresh from the bush when you're hiking the forests early in the autumn.

Should a Norwegian become a bit too boastful, you can always point out that the fork only became common in this country around 1850.

Sheep's head. Lefse, flatbrød and lapper. Potato dumplings with salted meat. Catch of the day.